DATA SEARCH

Light and Seeing

David Crystal and John Foster

Hodder & Stoughton

LONDON SYDNEY AUCKLAND TORONTO

Light and seeing

Our eyes are important, because they tell us about the shapes, colours, and sizes of all the things around us. We can see clearly only when there is enough light. At night, when it is very dark, it is difficult to see anything.

During the day, we can see things because the sun lights up the Earth. The sun produces a great deal of light, because it is so hot. When something gets very hot, it starts to make light. The first light it produces is red. We sometimes say that a thing is *red hot*. Electric fires are red hot.

As things get hotter, they become white hot. The sun is so hot that it is white hot. Right inside the sun, the temperature is about 15 million degrees Centigrade. The temperature of the parts that we see is about 6000°C.

Making light

Human beings have invented many ways of making light to help them to see when it is dark. To produce the heat needed for light, we can burn things to make flames. The first torches were burning pieces of wood.

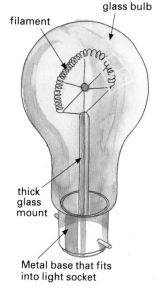

Later, candles were made. A piece of string was put in a bowl of wax, so that it would burn slowly. Flames are also used to make light in gas and oil lamps.

Today, we use electricity to make light inside an electric light bulb. If you put your hand near a lit bulb, you can feel that it is hot. The wire inside it is so thin that the electricity finds it difficult to pass through. This makes the wire get hot very quickly, and it glows white. The wire which gets hot is called a *filament*

Electricity is used to produce light in the neon signs you see in city centres. When electricity passes through neon gas, the neon produces a bright orange-red light.

Activities

1 List all the uses we make of electric light. How would your life be different without electric light?

2 Light can be used to send signals and give warnings. Talk about how light can be used in this way.

How light travels

When you switch on an electric torch, it makes a beam of light. If you want to use the torch to light up an object, you must point the torch in the right place. The light from the torch travels towards the object in straight lines.

We call these straight lines *light rays*. We can draw a light ray as a line with an arrow, like this:

light goes this way

Torches, searchlights, lighthouse lamps, and car headlights all make beams of light.

Light travels faster than anything else we know about. The sun is about 150 million kilometres away from the Earth. The light from the sun travels at 300 000 kilometres per second, and takes about eight minutes to reach the Earth.

Materials and light

Light can travel through some materials but not others. For example, light can travel through water, glass, and clear plastic. A material through which light can travel is said to be *transparent*
A material through which light cannot travel is said to be *opaque*
Certain materials allow just some of the light to pass through, such as frosted glass. A material which allows only some light to pass through is said to be *translucent*

The glass
in this window
is transparent.

The frosted glass
in this door
is translucent.
The wood is opaque.

4

Shadows

Because light travels in straight lines, it makes shadows. When an object is made of opaque materials, the light rays cannot pass through it. They can only get past on each side, so forming a shadow.

You can prove that light travels in straight lines by making shadow pictures on the wall in a dark room. Place a lamp so that it shines directly on a wall. Hold your hands between the wall and the beam of light. You can then make shadow pictures of birds and animals on the wall.

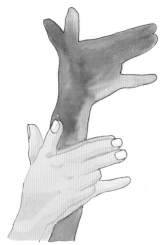

Refraction

Light travels at different speeds through different materials. It travels faster through air than through water. So, when a beam of light enters water, it slows down and is bent aside. This bending is called *refraction*. The picture shows a drinking straw in a glass of water. The straw looks broken, because the light rays are being refracted.

drinking straw

Activities

1 Collect materials and objects which you think are (a) transparent, (b) translucent, and (c) opaque. How can you check your ideas? Design an experiment to find out which materials and objects light can travel through.

2 Go out into the playground on a sunny day. Measure the length of your shadow at different times during the day. Does the length vary? Can you say why?

3 What is a sundial? How does it work? Can you design a simple sundial from a knitting needle, a piece of cardboard, and a cork?

Reflection

When light rays fall on a surface, some of the rays
bounce back. This is known as *reflection*, and we say
that the light is *reflected*. Shiny surfaces reflect
more light than other surfaces. For example, mirrors
reflect light because they have shiny surfaces.
Most mirrors are made of glass, which has been painted
silver on one side. Since light rays are straight,
we can change their direction quite easily
by using a mirror.

If you stand directly in front of a mirror, you
see yourself. Light rays bounce straight back.
You see a reflection of yourself.

If you stand to one side of the mirror, you see
things in other places. You see a reflection of
the table to your left.

Most objects cannot make their own light, but
they can reflect light. We can see the objects
around us because light is being reflected off them
into our eyes. At night-time, when it is dark,
objects are hard to see because so little light is
shining on them. When we switch on an electric light,
the objects reflect more light, so we can see them
more clearly.

Mirrors

Mirrors have many important uses. For example, car drivers need to know what is happening behind them, as well as in front. But when they are driving, it would be dangerous to turn their heads to look out of the back window. So a small mirror is fixed above the centre of the windscreen. The drivers can look in the mirror, and see a reflection of the road behind them, without turning their heads.

Sometimes words are written back to front on a vehicle, so that they can be read correctly in a car mirror. The word AMBULANCE may be painted on an ambulance back to front. When car drivers see it in their mirrors, they can read it, because writing is always back to front in a mirror.

Dentists' mirrors

Dentists look at your teeth by using a very small mirror on the end of a handle. They cannot look directly at the backs of your teeth, and they cannot put their heads right inside your mouth! Instead, they put a small mirror into your mouth, which helps them to see all parts of your teeth.

Periscopes

Sometimes we cannot see what we want to see by using only one mirror; so two mirrors are used. They are fixed at each end of a tube. The light rays change direction twice – once at one mirror, and again at the other mirror. This arrangement of mirrors is used in a *periscope*

Periscopes are used in submarines. The submarine can stay under water, and the crew are able to see what is happening on the surface by looking through a periscope.

Soldiers used simple periscopes during the First World War. The soldiers dug ditches, called *trenches*, to protect themselves from gun fire. They then used the periscopes to look out of the trenches, without having to raise their heads.

If a car or a lorry is towing a high load, such as a caravan, a periscope can be fixed on the car, so that the driver can see behind.

The girl is using a periscope which she made herself. Can you design and make a simple periscope?

rays of light

Curved mirrors

Not all mirrors are flat. Mirrors which bend in or out make things look peculiar. You may have been in a Hall of Mirrors at an amusement park. The rooms have lots of mirrors with all sorts of curves. When you look at them, you seem to be a funny shape.

Mirrors that curve inwards are called *concave* mirrors. Concave mirrors are used in torches and car headlights, to help make beams of light that point in one direction. The mirror, or *reflector*, is put behind the light bulb. All the light from the bulb is reflected in the same direction.

light goes all
round bulb

Light bulb without mirror.

The mirror, or reflector, is put behind the light bulb. All the light from the bulb is reflected in the right direction.

light reflected
in several directions

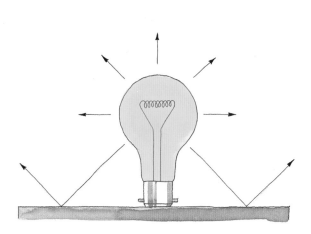

Light bulb with a flat mirror.

Light bulb with a curved mirror.

Activities

1 Look at your reflection in a polished spoon. Why does each side give a different reflection?
2 Print your name in capitals. Hold it in front of a mirror. Which letters look wrong?

3 ИWOⷩ TIƧ ƎƧAƎⷧꟼ What does this mirror message say?
Write your own mirror messages.
4 Talk about all the uses we make of mirrors.

Lenses and images

A lens is made of glass, plastic, or some other transparent substance, and is curved in shape. When light rays pass through a lens, the light rays change direction.

Lens shapes

A lens with a surface that curves inwards is called a *concave lens*. When light rays pass through a concave lens, they spread outwards.

A lens with a surface that curves outwards is called a *convex* lens. When light rays pass through a convex lens, they are bent inwards.

Cameras, projectors, telescopes, and microscopes all contain lenses, which bend the light that passes through them. We each have two lenses in our bodies, one in each eye.

Images

Light rays which pass through a lens form an *image* What you see reflected by a mirror is also called an image.

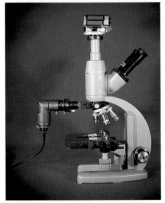

Magnifying glasses

The glass in a magnifying glass is a convex lens. A magnifying glass can be used to make small objects appear bigger. It can also be used to bend light rays towards one point, to produce an image.

The light rays of the sun can be bent towards one point by holding a magnifying glass so that the sun's rays shine through it. When the magnifying glass is held at a certain distance from the ground, a very bright spot of light is formed. The very bright spot is an image of the sun. We say that the light from the sun has been *focused* on this point. The distance between the lens in the magnifying glass and the image is called the *focal length* of the lens.

When we focus the sun's light, we focus its heat too. The sun's rays are so strong that a magnifying glass can be used to start a fire. A curved piece of glass from a bottle can act like a lens, and start a forest fire.

Hold a magnifying glass close to a page of print. If the page is less than the focal length away from the lens, the letters on the page appear to be bigger. The lens bends the light rays from each letter, so they appear to come from a larger image of the letter.

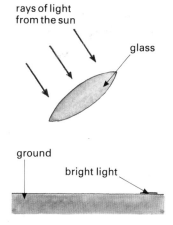

rays of light from the sun

glass

ground

bright light

Activities

1 Talk about what a lens is and what it does.
2 Make a list of objects which use a lens.

3 Look at a ruler through a magnifying glass. Explain why the numbers look bigger.
4 Look at pieces of different material through a magnifying glass, and talk about what you see.

How an eye works

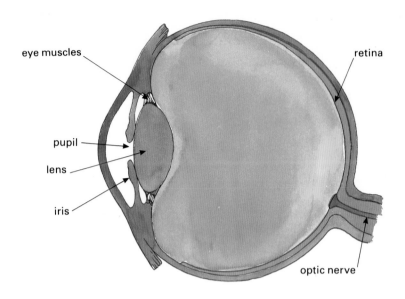

eye muscles

retina

pupil

lens

iris

optic nerve

Our eyes form tiny images of the world around us on a small screen inside each eye. The screen is called the *retina*. The eye is connected to the brain by a nerve called the *optic nerve*. This carries signals from the eye to the brain.

Light goes into the eye through a small hole called the *pupil*, which looks black. The part round the pupil is coloured, and is called the *iris*. The iris can be brown, grey, green, blue, or pink.

The light goes through the pupil to the lens, and then forms an image on the retina. People with good eyesight are able to read writing when it is close to their eyes, and can also see things far away. If we had a glass lens in our eyes, it would sometimes have to move closer to the retina, for the image to be clear. At other times, the lens would have to move away from the retina, to make a clear image.

If it is bright and sunny, the pupil looks small.

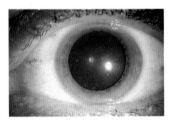

If it is dark, the pupil becomes bigger, allowing more light to pass into the eye.

In fact, the lens in an eye is made of a material that can change shape. It can form clear images of things at different distances from us. The muscles round the lens make it change shape. When the muscles change the shape of the lens, we say we are focusing our eyes.

A thick lens is needed to form a clear image of something close by:

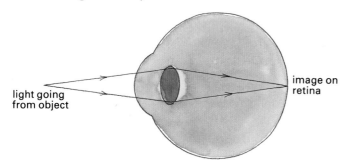

A thinner lens is needed to form a clear image of distant objects:

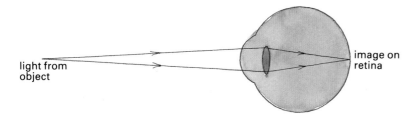

Activities

1 Stand where it is bright. Look at the size of a friend's pupils. Then, blindfold your friend for three minutes. Look at the pupils again. What do you notice?

2 Watch each other blinking. Talk about what happens. What do you notice?

3 Design some tests to find out which people in your class have the best eyesight. Draw a chart of your findings.

4 Imagine you meet a Martian. Explain what a human eye is and how it works.

People with poor eyesight

Not everyone has good eyesight. People with poor
eyesight wear glasses or contact lenses.

Some people cannot see near things clearly.
The muscles round their eyes cannot make the lenses
thick enough. They are said to be *long-sighted*.
They wear glasses with convex lenses in.

without glasses:

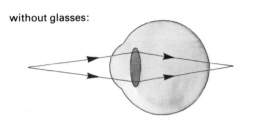

with glasses:

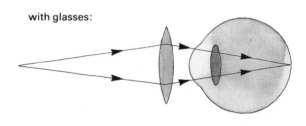

The image is out of focus.
The lens cannot bend
the light enough to form
a clear image on the retina.

The light from the object is
bent a little by the convex lens
before it reaches the eye's lens.
This makes up for the eye's lens
not bending the light rays enough.

Other people need glasses because the muscles
round their eyes cannot make the lens thin enough
for them to see distant objects clearly. These people
are said to be *short-sighted*. They wear glasses
with concave lenses.

without glasses:

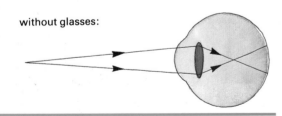

with glasses:

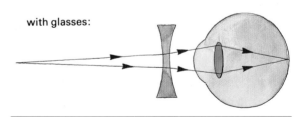

The image is out of focus.
The lens bends the light
too much, so that it does
not form a clear image
on the retina.

The light from the object is
bent a little by the concave lens
before it reaches the eye's lens.
This makes up for the eye's lens
bending the light rays too much.

Blindness

Every year in Britain, over 2000 people become blind. A few of them become blind as the result of an accident. Most of them lose their sight through some form of eye disease.

Blind people have to rely on their other senses. Many have guide dogs to help them. Because they cannot read ordinary books, special books are printed for them. The letters are printed as bumps which can be felt with the fingers. This special printing is called *braille*

Not all blind people can read braille. Many listen to tape books, which are tape-recordings of books being read aloud.

We each use one eye more than the other. Find out which eye you use most, by using both eyes to line up a pencil with the corner of the room. Then, close each eye in turn. When one eye is closed, the pencil seems to move to one side. The eye that is open when the pencil stays in line is your main eye.

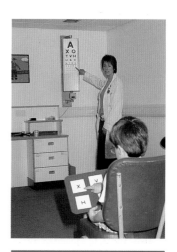

It is important to have your eyes tested regularly by a qualified optician.

Optical illusions

Even if we have good eyesight, our eyes can still make mistakes. Look at these pictures.

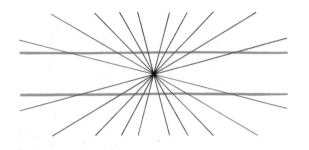

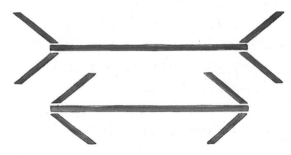

The two red lines look curved, but if you check them with a ruler, you will find that they are straight.

One line looks longer. Measure the lines with a ruler. What do you find?

Can you say why we think that the lines are curved, and why one line seems longer than the other?

The phantom sausage

Put the tips of your forefingers together in front of your face, level with your eyes. Focus your eyes on a distant object.

Keep looking at the object, and slowly move your fingers apart. Watch as a phantom sausage seems to float between your fingers.

What happens to the sausage if you close one eye?
Can you explain what the phantom sausage is?
Can you explain why we see the sausage?

Our eyes often play tricks on us. Tricks like these are called *optical illusions*

The hole in the hand

1 Make a long tube by rolling up a piece of paper, or find a long cardboard tube.
2 Hold the tube in your right hand, and put one end of the tube to your right eye.
3 Hold up your left hand with the palm facing you, and your little finger next to the other end of the tube.
4 Keep your left eye open, and look through the tube with your right eye.

Why do you think it looks as though there is a hole in the middle of your left hand?

A moving goldfish

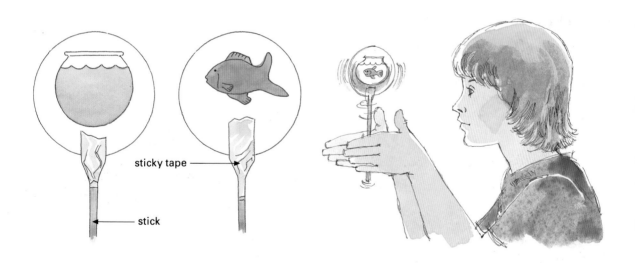

sticky tape

stick

Cut out a disc of white card. On one side, draw a picture of a goldfish. On the other side, draw a picture of a bowl of water.

Fix the card onto a stick. Rub the stick between your hands so that the card spins round. Watch the fish appear in the bowl.

Can you explain why it looks as if the fish is in the bowl?

Animal eyes

Animals with backbones have eyes which are very similar to human eyes. But the shape and size varies from animal to animal. The pupils of a cat's eyes are vertical slits, so it can see better up and down. The pupils of a horse's eyes are horizontal slits, so it can see better from side to side.

Animals which come out at night have large eyes to help them to see when there is not much light. Fish also have large eyes, to help them to see underwater.

Some animals, such as hawks and other birds of prey, have better eyesight than humans. But many animals cannot see colour. Cats, dogs, and rabbits cannot see colours. Animals which *can* see colours include birds, bees, snakes, lizards, and many fishes.

Insects have very different eyes from humans. A bee's eye consists of over 5000 tiny lenses. Each lens forms a separate image. The images are joined up by the bee's brain to make a complete picture. Eyes which consist of many separate lenses are known as *compound eyes*

A chameleon's eyes.

A horse fly's eyes.

A fish's eyes.

A cat's eyes.

Films

The optic nerve carries signals to the brain in a very short time. But if things happen too quickly, our eyes cannot work fast enough. They play tricks on us. When we watch a film at the cinema, or a programme on television, we are being fooled all the time.

The picture shows a short piece of cinema film. The film consists of lots of ordinary still pictures, or *frames*, joined together. Each frame is slightly different from the one before.

A film projector shows 24 different frames each second. One picture after another appears on the screen. But our eyes do not see 24 different separate pictures. The frames go by too quickly. The things that change position in the different frames seem to move on the screen.

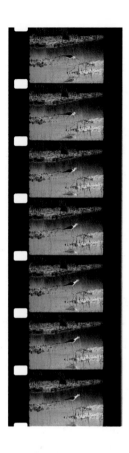

A pin-man book

The same thing happens when we flick through a pin-man book. Take an old exercise book. Draw a pin-man on the top right-hand corner of each page. Make each picture slightly different from the one before it. When you flick the pages with your finger, the man will appear to move.

How a camera works

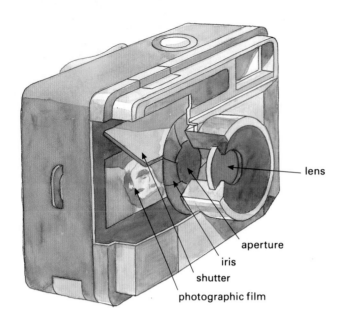

lens

aperture

iris

shutter

photographic film

A camera is rather like a mechanical eye. It uses a lens to make images on a roll of film. Cameras usually have a focus control, which can change the position of the lens. For long-distance photographs, the lens is moved closer to the film. For close-ups, the lens is moved further away. If the camera lens is not properly focused, photographs will be blurred.

Light does not reach the film in a camera all the time. There is a shutter, which is closed except when it is pressed to take a picture. The shutter then opens and closes very quickly. Light reaches the film, and makes an image.

On a dark day, it takes longer for a picture to be taken. The hole through which the light travels is known as the *stop*. The stop is opened wider, so that more light reaches the film. Otherwise the image on the film would be faint.

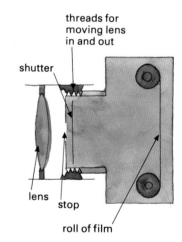

threads for moving lens in and out

shutter

lens

stop

roll of film

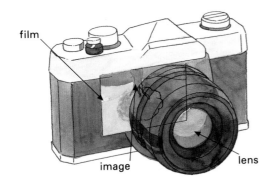

film

image   lens

A camera produces an upside-down image on the film.

A negative

The image produced on the film in a camera is upside-down. As the light rays pass through the lens, they are bent. The rays from the top of the scene fall onto the bottom part of the film.

The film is coated with chemicals which are sensitive to light, so an image of the scene is made on the film. In the film which is used for black and white photographs, the darkness on the image is reversed. The dark parts of the scene appear light, and the light parts appear dark.

When the film is taken out of the camera and developed, we get a *negative* image. If we then shine light through the negative onto special photographic paper, the black and white parts reverse again, to give a photograph with the correct shades. This is known as a *print*.

Activities

1 Draw a picture of the inside of a camera.
2 A camera is sometimes called a mechanical eye. Can you say why?

3 Prepare a short talk to explain what a camera does and how it works.

Colours

Light appears to be white, but in fact it is a mixture of different colours. The set of colours which make up light rays is called the *visible spectrum*. If sunlight shines through drops of water, a rainbow is sometimes formed. In a rainbow, you can see the colours of the visible spectrum.

   The British scientist, Isaac Newton (1642–1727), was very interested in colour. He proved that white light was really a mixture of colours, by passing light through a triangular block of glass, called a *prism* The light was split into a spectrum, like this:

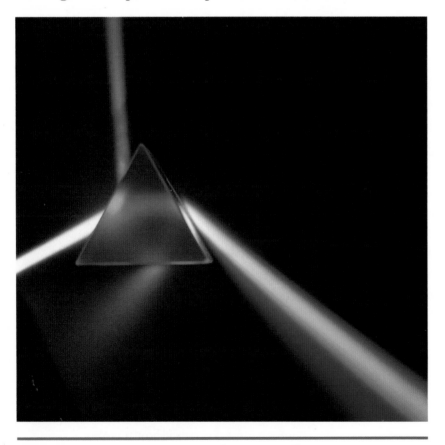

The colours of the spectrum are red, orange, yellow, green, blue, indigo, and violet.

Mixing colours

We can make the colours of the spectrum merge,
so that we see a white colour, if we make
a spinning disc of colour.

Make a Newton's disc

1 Cut out a cardboard disc with a 10 cm diameter.
2 Using a protractor, divide the disc into seven
equal sections.
3 Paint or colour each section a different colour
of the spectrum.
4 Make a hole in the centre of the disc, and push
a knitting needle through it.
5 Spin the disc as fast as you can.
When the disc spins very quickly, the colours merge.
We start to see only white.

Make a rainbow

On a sunny day, put a bowl of water by a window.
Lean a flat mirror against the inside of the bowl.
Draw the curtains, so that a thin beam of sunlight
shines onto the mirror. Then, hold a piece of white
card in front of the mirror, at the angle where
the sunlight is reflected off the mirror. You will
see a rainbow on the card.
The rainbow is formed because the 'wedge' of water
between the mirror and the surface of the water
is acting like a prism.

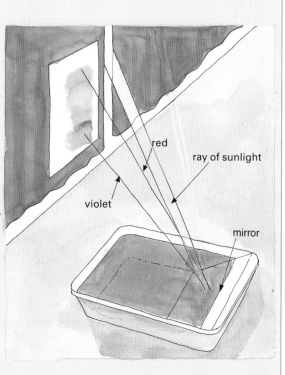

red

ray of sunlight

violet

mirror

Primary colours of light

White light can be made from just three colours – red, green, and blue. These are known as the *primary colours* of light. All the main colours can be made by mixing the primary colours together.

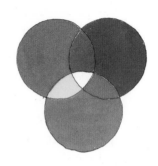

Colour television

Colour television pictures are made by mixing the primary colours. The screen consists of millions of dots. Some dots can be made to glow red; some glow green; and some glow blue. The dots are so small and so close together that the naked eye does not see each one separately.

The colour on different parts of the screen changes when different dots glow at the same time. If all the dots glow, the picture will be white. If two types of dot glow, they give light like this:

red and green makes yellow
green and blue makes blue/green
blue and red makes purple

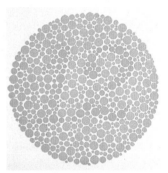

Colour blindness

Some people are unable to tell the difference between certain colours. This is called *colour blindness*. Most people who are colour blind can see only two basic colours. Colour blindness affects more men than women. In Europe about 8 out of every 100 people are colour blind.

The illustration is an example of a pattern that is used to test for colour blindness.

Coloured paints

The primary colours of paints are not the same as the primary colours of light. This is because paints only reflect light. They do not produce light, as the sun or a TV set does. The primary colours of paints are red, yellow, and blue. They can be mixed together to make most other colours.

The coloured pictures in books are made by mixing these colours. Like the picture on a TV screen, each picture consists of lots of tiny dots.

Objects look coloured because of the way they reflect the colours of the spectrum. For example, a blue T-shirt reflects more blue than any other colour, and absorbs most of the other colours shining on it.

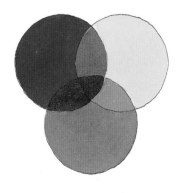

Activities

1 What happens when you mix two different colours of paint? Experiment with different mixtures, and make a chart of your findings.
2 Use a magnifying glass to study the coloured pictures in a book. What do you see?

3 Make a pair of cardboard spectacles. Experiment with lenses of different coloured plastic or cellophane. How do things look different, depending on the colour of the lens?

Telescopes

Very distant objects can be made to look nearer, if you look at them through a telescope or binoculars. Scientists who study the stars are called *astronomers*. Astronomers need telescopes to study the stars and planets.

The sun is the nearest star to Earth. It produces so much light that it is very dangerous to look at using an ordinary telescope or through binoculars. The brightness would damage your eyes. Scientists have to use telescopes with special lenses.

The stars are so hot that they produce their own light. Anything that makes light, or reflects light towards Earth, can be studied using telescopes with lenses and mirrors.

Planets and moons do not make their own light, but we can still see them through a telescope. We see them because light from the sun is reflected back towards the Earth. They act like gigantic mirrors. The diagram shows how we see the moon.

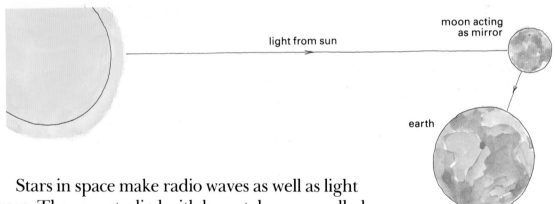

light from sun

moon acting as mirror

earth

Stars in space make radio waves as well as light rays. They are studied with large telescopes called *radio telescopes*. Radio telescopes do not have lenses, but usually have steel surfaces to reflect the radio waves.

The first proper telescope was designed in 1609 by an Italian scientist called Galileo. He had heard that things seemed larger when they were looked at through two lenses. So he fitted two lenses into a lead pipe, one at each end. His first telescope made things look three times larger. Later, he made telescopes with improved lenses that made things look over 30 times larger.

How to make a telescope

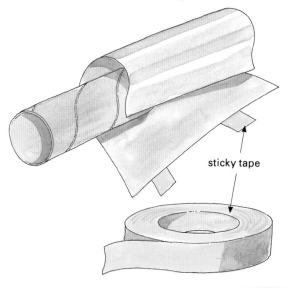

sticky tape

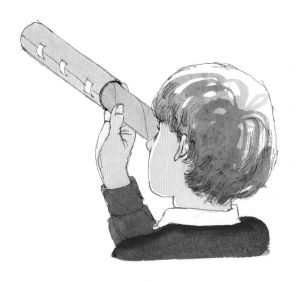

Find a cardboard tube about 25 cm long. Using sticky tape and card, make another tube which is slightly wider, so that the cardboard tube fits tightly inside it.

Use glue to fix a convex lens at one end of the wider tube, and a concave lens at one end of the narrower tube. Then slide the open end of the narrow tube into the open end of the wide tube. You look through the end of the narrower tube.

Use your telescope to look at the moon and other distant objects. Focus it by sliding the narrower tube in and out until you get a clear picture.

Can you suggest what difference it would make if you used a convex lens for the eyepiece instead of a concave lens?

Microscopes

Even with perfect eyesight, and in daylight,
there are still many things that we cannot see.
We have to use special instruments to study them.

Very small things can be seen through a *microscope*
A microscope makes things look bigger. Scientists
often use microscopes in their research. Biologists,
for example, use microscopes to magnify tiny
creatures and parts of other living things.

Collect some mini-beasts and study them using
a microscope. Talk about and record what you see.

A simple microscope

Make a hole about 2.5 cms in diameter in a piece
of card. Stick a piece of sellotape over the hole.
With a drinking straw, put a drop of water onto
the sellotape.

Look at some writing through the drop of water.
The water acts like a lens, and the writing looks
bigger.

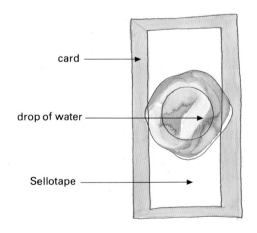

card

drop of water

Sellotape

Invisible rays

Light rays can be seen with our eyes. They form the visible spectrum. But there are other rays, which are invisible. These other rays travel as fast as light, but can be detected only with special equipment. Some of them play important parts in our lives. The table shows a list of them and what they do.

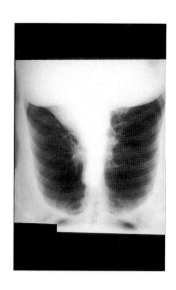

Type of ray
Radio wave: Carries radio and TV messages
Radar: Detects solid objects
Infra-red light: Carries heat
Ultra-violet: Present in sunlight; helps to cause sunburn
X-ray: Used to take photographs inside our bodies

Some of these rays can be photographed with special cameras. Infra-red rays are an example. These are produced by anything warm. We make infra-red rays when our bodies are warmer than the air outside.

Infra-red cameras are used to search for people who may have been buried alive during an avalanche or earthquake.

This photgraph was taken with an infra-red camera. It shows the shape of warm things, even when they cannot be seen with the naked eye.

Crossword

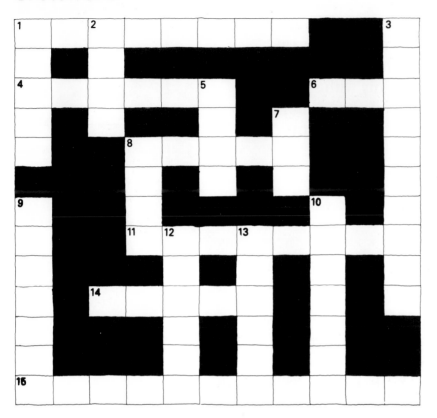

Clues across

1 The thin wire that glows white inside an electric light bulb (8)

4 Type of lens used in glasses for people who are long-sighted (6)

6 Things glow white when they get very ____ (3)

8 The picture formed by an object in front of a mirror or lens (5)

11 It consists of the seven bands of colour seen in a rainbow (8)

14 Newton used one to separate the colours in 11 across (5)

15 You can see through these materials (11)

Clues down

1 The muscles in our eyes help us to do this so that we can see objects clearly (5)

2 There is one in each eye and at each end of a telescope (4)

3 A person who studies the stars (10)

5 Photograph taken with an invisible ray (1–3)

7 A primary colour (3)

8 Round, coloured part of the eye (4)

9 What a mirror can do to light (7)

10 A special type of printing for the blind (7)

12 You can make these from negatives (6)

13 What you use to take photographs (6)

Glossary

concave (p.10) curving inwards at the centre,
as in some kinds of mirror or lens

convex (p.10) curving outwards at the centre,
as in some kinds of mirror or lens

filament (p.3) a thin thread of material, such as wire,
used in electric light bulbs

focus (p.11) the point at which light rays meet,
after their direction has been changed

image (p.10) a picture formed by an object
in front of a mirror or lens

iris (p.12) the round, coloured part of the eye,
which surrounds the pupil

lens (p.10) a piece of curved glass which makes
light rays change direction

magnify (p.11) to make something appear larger
than it really is

periscope (p.8) a long tube containing two mirrors,
placed in such a way that people can see above
them or round corners

prism (p.22) a three-sided block of glass which breaks up
white light into different colours

pupil (p.12) the small, black, round opening in the centre
of the eye, which allows light to enter

reflection (p.6) the throwing back of light rays,
as by a mirror

retina (p.12) the area at the back of the eye
which is sensitive to light

visible spectrum (p.22) the colours that make up
white light

Index